Sea Shells and Sand Castles

Sea Shells and Sand Castles

Jeffrey Jay Niehaus

RESOURCE *Publications* • Eugene, Oregon

SEA SHELLS AND SAND CASTLES

Copyright © 2021 Jeffrey Jay Niehaus. All rights reserved. Except for brief quotations in critical publications or reviews, no part of this book may be reproduced in any manner without prior written permission from the publisher. Write: Permissions, Wipf and Stock Publishers, 199 W. 8th Ave., Suite 3, Eugene, OR 97401.

Resource Publications
An Imprint of Wipf and Stock Publishers
199 W. 8th Ave., Suite 3
Eugene, OR 97401

www.wipfandstock.com

PAPERBACK ISBN: 978-1-6667-3406-5
HARDCOVER ISBN: 978-1-6667-2952-8
EBOOK ISBN: 978-1-6667-2953-5

VERSION NUMBER 101421

FOR MAGGI

who endured Florida

CONTENTS

LAKE WORTH BEACH | 1

SUNBURN | 2

SUN TAN | 3

𝕳𝖆𝖓𝖘𝖊𝖑 𝖚𝖓𝖉 𝕲𝖗𝖊𝖙𝖊𝖑 | 4

EUROPEAN SUBTROPICS | 5

WATER ROCKET | 6

SUNDAY MORNING AT NORTH PALM BEACH | 7

AS PALM BEACH INLET WAS | 8

EVENING STAR | 9

CONCH | 10

SEA TURTLE ON SAND | 11

A REQUEST | 12

BRAIN CORAL | 13

INTERLOPER | 14

CLOUDSCAPE | 15

ISLAMORADA | 16

WATER WATER WATER | 17

AN ONLY | 18

INK INK INK INK | 19

EFFORTLESS | 20

LUNCH AND ART | 21

WRONG SOMEHOW | 22

SCARLET CONCLAVE | 23

A SONG | 24

SANDY CONCH | 25
KIAWAH | 26
TWO MILLS | 27
BIRCH AQUARIUM | 28
PRUNING | 29
WHY WORRY? | 30
AFLOAT OFF LAKE WORTH BEACH | 31
MARBLES | 32
CUMULUS MOON | 33
EZRA POUND AND I | 34
PIG HEADED FATHER | 35
SHARK ROUND UP | 36
NO PRESSURE | 37
PARROT JUNGLE | 38
FLORIDA | 39
SPINY PUFFER | 40
SET SAIL | 41
SEA CUCUMBER OFF KEY WEST | 42
EDGAR LEE MASTERS | 43
CAPE ANN BREWING CO. | 44
WATER MOCCASIN | 45
LOXAHATCHEE CANOE | 46
ATTITUDES / LATITUDES | 47
A SKEPTIC | 48
YUKON GOLD | 49
A PORTUGUESE WRECK | 50
NOCTURNAL DIVE | 51
COCONUT BOYS | 52
SCHUMANN NOVELETTE | 53
ESSAY ON CRITICISM | 54

BRONZE BOLT | 55

SCHWEINSHAXE | 56

JAMAICA COCONUT | 57

MENTOR | 58

SOUTHERN BOULEVARD | 59

TRISTAN AMONG BUTTERCUPS | 60

STONE | 61

WATERSPOUT | 62

KUMQUATS | 63

A BOYHOOD HALLOWEEN | 64

SHALLOWS | 65

MORAY EEL | 66

IF A COTTAGE | 67

AFTER SCHOOL | 68

OHIO FLASHBACK | 69

GENERAL OFFICERS | 70

T. E. LAWRENCE | 71

SOME PHILOSOPHY | 72

THEOLOGY I | 73

THEOLOGY II | 74

CASA ROBUSTA | 75

LANTANA SCHOOL | 76

CANEM AMANS | 77

LATIN DAY | 78

TRIMMING HEDGE | 79

SAND | 80

APPOINTMENT | 81

TROLDHAUGEN | 82

MAGIC CARPET | 83

LUNCH UNDER AN UMBRELLA | 84

BUDDHA BODHISSATVA | 85

WALKING TRISTAN | 86

ANGEL BLUSH | 87

COASTAL IDYLL | 88

AFTER ALL | 89

KEY CASAS | 90

SCROLL UPON SCROLL | 91

PENDULUM | 92

DARK AND LIGHT | 93

RAFT RENTAL | 94

A BURDEN, A GIFT | 95

WAVES | 96

BEACH BOY | 97

SEA SHELLS | 98

SAND CASTLES | 99

SEA SHELLS AND SAND CASTLES | 100

LAKE WORTH BEACH

When I was young

                        and you also

Young world young ocean
No harm to you or me
From north or down south
Now all upended as you may
A cart of coconuts

SUNBURN

Down to Daytona
Hot summer day
On the beach

I lay and saw
A lovely girl
And lay too long

And afterward
A lobster look
Body so hot

SUN TAN

On a beach
Lake Worth
Palm Beach

On a towel
Our back yard
Our front yard

Cutting grass
On a bike
On a walk

HÄNSEL UND GRETEL

Go among trees
Gingerbread house
Cookie folk stand
Once took air
And

        in Oberammergau

A mural

Vor Hexen nehmt euch fein in Acht:
Seht, was sie mit dem Hänsel macht!

EUROPEAN SUBTROPICS

Debussy Turina Falla
Captured Iberia or Seville
Nocturnal gardens or

        Sombrero de tres picos

I could don and be
A Spanish don in

        a *jardín*

A *hacienda* now

        flowers

Valencia Lantana red rose

        Bougainvillea

Perfume

    nuestra noche

WATER ROCKET

Pumped you up
Blue oval
Four fins

Ad astra per aspera

Palm Springs
Our front yard
After Christmas
Turkey

Thirteen
South of

          Canaveral

SUNDAY MORNING AT NORTH PALM BEACH

Sunday   not long

                before dawn

Luminous staterooms—portals
Out of vanquished darkness announce
A major cruise ship
Mouth of Palm Beach Inlet and
Peanut Island

                Port of Palm Beach

Walk north and I see
Under a gazebo

                a cluster

Palm Beach Atlantic youths

                sunrise

About to pray

AS PALM BEACH INLET WAS

A crane stood rusty solitary

Above some rocks at Port of Palm Beach

Rocky arms stretched east and west

And braced the shore against a deep cut

An inlet where pelagian craft

Cargo boats full of consumer goods

Tankers full of oil or gasoline

Boston whalers ordinary speedboats

Charter boats sailboats galore

Also rubber rafts navigated

Toward our Intracoastal Waterway

Around Peanut Island and to port

EVENING STAR

Orb uninhabitable

You orbit so close to the sun
Atmosphere hot carbon dioxide
Your atmospheric pressure would crush
A submarine's hull

                Nothing

Could live on you

Alone

Purple sky

CONCH

Conch O

        inward

Sunset colors

        yellow pink mauve

Splendorous beyond
Many volume *Kirkliche Dogmatik*
Any biblical theology

Sunset in you

        articulates

More than learned pen
Scholar's quill

Silly goose
Knows ink

        and paper

SEA TURTLE ON SAND

So young

        upside down

After a storm you lay
Portuguese Man o' War

Out of your beak
Venomous tentacles

        hung

One repast too many

        rigor mortis

A REQUEST

An I may I'd have
A long afternoon

      and hear

A serenade of small waves
A low breeze

      as though

Atlantic were a large Aeolian harp
And I a solitary auditor

Beauty all about

      and you

Young woman

      blonde hair

Fondled by

      enamored wind

BRAIN CORAL

Coral reef park

                        Pennekamp

June air hot above
Warm water

                  accommodates

Cold below a thermocline

Inhale and buoyant

                      arc above

Fissured brain coral
Full of savvy
Above

               scholars

Exhale and float

                     down

Toward bare sand

INTERLOPER

Stumps of Palm Beach pier

                                  I swam among

Warm ocean turquoise
Undulant sand

                    a few broken shells

Ocean bottom unaffected
By a scuba diver

Saucer shaped bubbles wobble upward

And a form

Lucent out of green haze

                              barracuda

CLOUDSCAPE

Summer thunder shower

                            and after

Wet steamy earth, and sky
Azure blue
Sunny clouds mount up
A place I haply study
Unpolluted by the world
Or those who walk on't

                             contemplate

Or better

ISLAMORADA

Below Key Largo
Below Tavernier
Island flora, turquoise shallows

Florida Straits—have me
A warm embrace

Thy

Unparalleled oblivious way

Obliviscor
Sol after sol

Until no more days

Stroll on sand among shells
Offered by waves

Et ego nauta
Aut nautilus

WATER WATER WATER

For Paul M

Dark water under a canoe
And you stroke fluidly
Unfathomable lake

Pellucid ocean of Palm Beach
You move aquatically
Conversant with guitarfish

O fluency of water
You also watery
In your brave composition

AN ONLY

On your coast
No care no attitude
An afternoon
Under palm fronds

Coconuts pendant
A warm breeze
Off the 'Glades
Southern comfort

Below

    a slope

Rollers

Ineffable

    harmonia

INK INK INK INK

Luther threw an inkwell it is said
At the Devil

        and so

All the holy words the ink would say
Stopped Satan

Scholar afterward
Goes to war
OCEANS OF INK

On a sandy floor
An octopus escapes
A cloud of ink

A squid also
No bigger than
Your thumb

EFFORTLESS

Bay window and afternoon sun
At my back and ahead
Träumerei

Palm Beach and Flagler's mansion
Intracoastal
Monikers from Florida

Words of Florida

Waves, conch shells, palm trees

Almost a poem

LUNCH AND ART

Over a table at Ceres Bakery
You and I had coffee and
Small lunch

        Sandwiches, pickles

Ordinary fare but

        more rare

Talk of art — did Beethoven know joy
At the creative moment
As I would say

        An inner dance

As poetry arose within
At your harmonious moment of performance
Or practicing a duet?

Poet and pianist both are souls
Whose inner dance emerges
For a public.

WRONG SOMEHOW

As though a dog were found
Atop a poplar

As though a dugong
Rode a pony

So an honors convocation
Awards and all that

SCARLET CONCLAVE

"To thin the scarlet conclave of old men"
—John Keats

Spring cardinals, not we
Nor those among us who
Sport Harvard regalia for the nonce

But in multicolored glad rags
Down an aisle we walk
Procession self-important more than a little

Fathers and mothers overawed
Grandparents
And children also watch

Pomp and Circumstance normally
A trumpet voluntary
Rows of students

Graduate into a larger world
Steps eager or unsure

—a vision

A SONG

Sunny afternoon and hot
Quartz sand of Lake Worth
Also hot underfoot

I lay on a beach towel
And she so close
She loved horses

I rode only once
Among saw grass
Got saddle sores

She was

                like Florida

Uncomplicated

SANDY CONCH

Slowly out of sand
Pulled by a youth's hand
A hollow conch

Sand flowed away

Underwater cloud

A lot of small holes

Sea change

KIAWAH

for Kristen Ashley

Ashley River close
Isle whose name
Come of Indians
Almost forgot

Kiawah
Pure quartz sand
Warm turquoise shallows
West Beach Village

Sand pipers, sea gulls
Alligators on the prowl
Bobcats curious
About

              us

At sunset
Waves lap

            full moon

TWO MILLS

Small windmill
Hard by *Sanssouci*

Bothered the sleep of
Friedrich der Große

Yerba Buena
Creek
Fruitful sawmill

Then

Gold fever

A mill

and

A mill

BIRCH AQUARIUM

Above water
Day after Christmas
Partly cloudy

Palm trees far below
Tall, slender, crowned with fronds
Small oases

Slender forms

Some in wetsuits

Subtropical flourish

                      in

Austere air

Above
Saltwater tanks
Dark halls

Sea anemones

Sea horses

PRUNING

Today
No rhapsody
Or transport

Only as a gardener
Comes to prune
So plants may grow

More productive
So I today
Come to prune

A word here
A line there

WHY WORRY?

Months of sand
And no sea

A boat seems to float
On no wave

A boat afloat
On air

And now
MARE SECUNDUM

And now
ECCE:

AFLOAT OFF LAKE WORTH BEACH

Afloat
A pier not far away
Decades old

Sway backed

Warm water
Above the thermocline

Solar mood

MARBLES

Dark green vase
From a florist

A temporary home

O so many marbles

Boulders, cat's eyes
Flowers caught

Eternally in glass
All for me

A summer afternoon

A neighbor's gift

CUMULUS MOON

A warm Florida evening
Mother and I

A long walk

Some conversation

We looked up

Cumulus tower
Giant above
Serene

Afloat

Sublunary

Almost a model

EZRA POUND AND I

"I picked up a collection of Pound's poetry recently and this particular poem piqued my interest. I love the rhythm and emotion of it, but have a very hazy idea of what's going on."
—Online blogger.

Join the company!

Some giftedness for language, certainly,
A turn of phrase
There, here a colorful image
And those ineluctable allusions;
Languages ancient, modern, foreign
As though our mother tongue were not enough

(It suited greater poets pretty well).

So, a prosaic poem on Ezra Pound,
Who was nathless my personal door
To poetry at Cross Keys High in Buckhead.

I wrote Cantos before I graduated
And years later came back to poetry
But not to Pound.

PIG HEADED FATHER

What tiresome stuff
You solitary dog

Although a dog's too good a moniker
Wagging your democratic haunches

To borrow an aristocratic phrase
From Turgenev

Pound had you figured out
Although he followed you

And William Carlos Williams who mistook
Your mediocrity for liberation

From iambic pentameter's tyranny
And so you gave

Poetic license to a challenged crowd
Who could hardly produce one lovely line

Although you gave them democratic freedom
To make as though they were poets somehow.

SHARK ROUND UP

South of Palm Beach Inlet
Forty, fifty yards

Calm sea sunny afternoon
Twenty foot depth

Our twenty foot Boston Whaler
Rocked mildly and we

Parked beside a shoal
Of Spanish mackerel when suddenly

Two sharks, dark silhouettes
Come in swiftly and surround

The panicked mackerel
As though two cowboys

Rode herd and surgically
One shark and then another

Took turns and sliced
And harvested

Mackerel leapt into the air
Out of frothy water

NO PRESSURE

No pressure
To squeeze out a word

No pressure
To squeeze out a verse

Blood
From a turnip

Water
From a dry well

Only what comes
Today

And
Tomorrow

PARROT JUNGLE

Parrot jungle
Or bold cockatoos

Splashes of color
Jamaican sun splash

Only in Miami
Subtropical home

Carib sanctuary
Of the sun

Cockatoo imports
At home

Flamingos
Floridian too

FLORIDA

Florida venereal soil
So Wallace Stevens

As in Venus
Aphrodite

On a clam shell?
Or Atlantic

Love of shells
Ashore in wet sand

Love of small lizards
On stucco walls

In warm sunlight
In winter

Love of ochre tiles
Spanish architecture

Human color added
At home

SPINY PUFFER

Color of cream
Off Lake Worth pier

Aware you swam
Saw a snorkeler

And full of ocean
Awesome now

Abrupt spines
Bulging eyes

Maritime warning
To any man

Imago Dei notwithstanding
Stand off

SET SAIL

A forty foot yacht
Becalmed

On turquoise water
In the Keys

Up from a reef
Scuba tank dries

In warm sun and I
Would be

Full of sun and sea
And want no shore

Shore far away
Nonetheless supplies

Needful stuff
For a vagabond

SEA CUCUMBER OFF KEY WEST

Late afternoon
Lonely beach

To avoid haze
Spat on my face plate

And now among
Swaying sea grass

Almost camouflaged
A soft animal

Called a vegetable
Often

Garnish for some
Aquatic salad

Sea cucumber
And later

Altocumulus sunset
Coral red

EDGAR LEE MASTERS

"Did you ever hear of Editor Whedon giving to the public treasury any of the money he received for supporting candidates in office?"

or

Did you ever hear of Editor Whedon
Giving to the public treasury any of the money he received
For supporting candidates in office?

CAPE ANN BREWING CO.

"Cape Ann Brewing Company Lowers its Sails for Good."
—*Eater Boston*, Jan. 20, 2020, 12:03 p.m.

Airy pub
Patio, wooden tables
Umbrella shade
On a wharf

On a bay
Lobster crates
Fishing boats
Afternoon

Shrimp plate
Calamari
Oyster sandwich
Haddock

Cask Ale
Bald Seagull
Maiden Voyage
Captain Red Face

Sun and clouds
Sea gull cries
Echoes
Echoes

WATER MOCCASIN

Fourteen year old
A cane pole

Able fisherman
At Lake Osborne

On a concrete drain
Hot afternoon

July after lunch
Lazy feet dangle

I look down
Under brown water

Umber yellow bands
Sinuous alive

Swam beneath my feet
Silent warning

LOXAHATCHEE CANOE

Wooden tables above,
A picnic lunch

Down a slope
Aluminum canoes

At the ready.
Loxahatchee

Brown and strong
Tannin and tide

And now a paddle
Westward, upstream

Hug the bank
Strong contrary flow

Primordial river
Unmastered

But a tributary
No challenge

Smooth water
Spanish moss

On a bank
A wild boar

ATTITUDES / LATITUDES

"My North is leafless and lies in a wintry slime
Both of men and clouds."
—Wallace Stevens

And so sail on high ship
To a land of bare trees
Almost half the year and then
A mind of winter at the heart of it

You love winter and its nothingness
Nothingness of men in overcoats
Nothingness of filthy weather
Slime of men in crowds

Away from opalescent seas,
Coralline, and marly bottoms seen
Easily from a yawl afloat
Just above trade winds

Go, embrace null and know
Snowfall smothers all under its blanket —
Not Florida, her shores and warm breezes,
Unfathomable shoals

A SKEPTIC

Modern or postmodern
Educated or
Tutored in a certain way

Lucid and good, trenchant and worthy
After all
Alien to you

Primordial, epic metanarrative
And you
Closed

Would not engage beyond
A secondary
Incredulity

Come from others
Justified from others
Yourself unjustified

YUKON GOLD

Yukon savvy, Yukon gold
Yukon stories to be told

Yukon sunsets cold and free
Yukon busts like Sam McGee
Who found his way from Tennessee
To Service's cre-ma-tory

A PORTUGUESE WRECK

Off Palm Beach
Two miles or so
Eighteen feet deep by sonar

Undulant sand
Molded by waves
And a dark outline

Black and black ribs
Arc upward
Broken off

And down we go
A student and I
From Palm Beach Atlantic College

Sunk by hurricane
Four hundred years ago
Tempestade tropical

NOCTURNAL DIVE

Nocturnal dive
Off Marathon Key

Underwater flashlight
Canyon of coral

At the bottom
Crowd of sea urchins

Venomous
Long purple spines

Crackling sound
Of snapping shrimp

Alpheidae, Oligocene
Primordial almost

But older
A nurse shark

COCONUT BOYS

West Palm Beach 1957
Two young colored men
Fallen coconuts
After storm

A truck
Crawls along
Lakeland Drive
Gathering

A windfall
For them

I watch
Ohio boy

SCHUMANN NOVELETTE

Afternoon audience
Sunbeams in the hall
Jonathan Edwards College
Motes in the air

You played Schumann
Was it Opus 21, #8?
And for a moment Yale
Overflowed with sound

Warm Romantic music
Neue Bahnen
Back then
Now accustomed

Beautiful because accustomed
Accustomed because beautiful
A sound to recall
In winter.

ESSAY ON CRITICISM

      I

After Aristotle
After Horace
Pope essayed
To show us how, how not

      II

A palm frond
A sand flea
A sandpiper
Shows the way

BRONZE BOLT

Wooden pier
Eighth grade
Lake Worth Junior High

On Saturdays
I swam around
Snorkeled too

Also walked
Along your planks
Among the fishermen

A twenty something
Walked among your ruins

On the beach
Wooden shards
One bronze bolt

I pulled it out
Gave it to a friend

SCHWEINSHAXE

"Your soul will delight in the richest of fare."
—Isa 55:2

Pig knuckle
At Heinrich's

Crispy skin
Juicy

Marinated
Adored flavor

Beer and a friend
Good times

Evocative
Of Bayern

JAMAICA COCONUT

Dusty morning crowd
Spanish Town Road
80+ degrees

January

A coconut stand
Cool box
Tall vendor
Straw hat

Chill coconut
One machete swipe
Open fruit
A cool drink

MENTOR

Odysseus
Gave you
Care of young
Telemachus —

Young man
Unpresuming
A gray-eyed goddess
At his side —

Your lad and Odysseus
Took home back

Mentor now
A common noun

SOUTHERN BOULEVARD

Autumn, 1957
We drove past
Palm Beach Air Force Base
Meadow Park School
Our goal

B-47s, C-124s
Smaller craft
A boy
Fell in love

Oceanward
Across the Intracoastal
Bath and Tennis Club
Uncommon rotary
Marjorie Merriweather Post's
Mar-a-Lago

TRISTAN AMONG BUTTERCUPS

Donald Duck's cousin
Gladstone Gander
Lucky bird

Sallied forth
Sun sang love songs
To buttercups

Good dog
Sunny day
Amble

On dewy grass
Among buttercups
Morning snap

STONE

On a table
Large or small

Stable you
Above all

Nor do you
Exfoliate

Today
Nor do I

WATERSPOUT

Lake Worth Beach
Dark stormy clouds
Sultry summer day

A sudden cone
Supple dips
Almost writhes

Cloud to sea
More and more defined
Atlantic tornado

Churns water
Far away
Far away

KUMQUATS

I

Woven basket
Of kumquats
From: West Palm Beach
To: Martins Ferry

From grandma to me
Oval suns
Shone out
A green jungle

Mid-December
Ohio snow

II

Arboreal
Kumquats
Lake Park
Our back yard

Orange ovals
Show
Morning glory
Among green leaves

Mid-December
Florida

A BOYHOOD HALLOWEEN

On darkling Halloween
A young skull and bones
Romped across our yard
And down North Seventh Street.
Spooks and hobgoblins,
Draculas and ghouls
Witches and warlocks
Buccaneers at large
And random royalty
Dukes and dunces
Scholars and nobles
A poet, a sage,
A soldier
A space man
A sailor
And more
A panoply of characters galore
Laughed from door to door
And made our road a stage.

SHALLOWS

    I

Beige sand
Turquoise shallows

Eleven year old

I snorkeled
And discovered

Grains of sand
Shell fragments

    II

At pier's end
Below the thermocline

Twenty years older

Scuba man
I explored

Quiet floor

MORAY EEL

Palm Beach Inlet
Tumbled rocks
North side
Down under

Dappled sun and shade
As clouds blew by above

Suddenly in sunlight
Head and face
Full of danger

Out of a hole
In pale stone

IF A COTTAGE

A cottage
Composed
Of bamboo, palm frond thatch

At Sugarloaf
Bahia Honda
Sunset Key

Rattan table
In shade
Soft breezes

Open door
Sand and sea
Under foot and beyond

Coconut meat
Snapper
Sea grape wine

AFTER SCHOOL

Home from
Lake Worth High
A snack

Cold chicken
Potato chips
Coke or Pepsi

Village of Palm Springs
Paper route
Comes

After
Channel 7's
Popeye Club

OHIO FLASHBACK

Sun cascaded in
And I awoke to Easter
And an Easter egg hunt
In our living room.
I sought and found
A chocolate Easter bunny
Under a sofa,
Chocolate crème-file eggs
Under a cushion
And jelly beans
Wrapped in plastic bags
Behind a radio.
Before that joy could fade
We played
A game with colored eggs
Mom had made.
We cracked
End against end:
Slim versus slim,
Fat versus fat,
And now,
Once all were cracked,
We ate them,
And that was that.

GENERAL OFFICERS

Alexander at the Punjab
Caesar   in Britain
Cornwallis at Yorktown
Napoleon at Moscow
Rommel at El Alamein
Lee at Gettysburg

Success or failure
What they fought for
Their cultures
Now long gone
Their wars hardly known
To our high school graduates
Their honored dead
Not remembered

Our faulty public education
Blameless

T. E. LAWRENCE

"Wisdom has built her house,
She has hewn her seven pillars."
—Prov 9:1

Seven Pillars of Wisdom —
A Triumph
He called it

Could he see now
Fruit of blood
Hundreds of miles
Of solar glare
A sherif gone sun-blind
Fetid wells
Louse-covered sleep

Exploded railroads
Bloated Turk bodies

Pan-Arab
Fantasy

SOME PHILOSOPHY

        I

What does not exist
Is not

A thought of what does not exist
May be
      — Plato

        II

What does not exist
Is not

A thought of what does not exist
May be
      — Descartes

THEOLOGY I

Matter is
An illusion of mortal mind
    —Mary Baker Eddy

Matter is
A product of divine mind
    —God

THEOLOGY II

Sin is
The concrete form of Nothingness
      — Karl Barth

Sin is
All that is not of faith
      — God

CASA ROBUSTA

Orange tree
Our back yard
Grapefruit tree
Our front yard
Kumquat tree
At the side

Spanish style
Umber roof tiles
Stucco walls —
And inside
Terrazzo floors
Rattan furniture

Fruitful outside
Sane inside

Our home
South Florida

LANTANA SCHOOL

Old wooden floors
Dark wood desks
Inkwell holes

Hall door open
Morning air

Down the hall
Music from one office
Sound of sea gulls

Outside
Coconut palms

Ohio boy
Come down
Paradise

CANEM AMANS

"A righteous man knows the nature of his animal."
—Prov 12:10

Amicae

Love your God
Love your dog

The second command
Follows the first

As day
Follows dawn

As growth
Follows gentle rain

One touch,
Faster heartbeat

One look,
Wagging tail

Who is more blessed
The lover or the loved?

LATIN DAY

Lake Worth High
Sophomore year
Latin Day

Boys wore togas
Girls wore stolas

End of day
Procession downtown

Then disband
Wander about

Enter our library
A newsstand

Wondering looks

TRIMMING HEDGE

Palm Beach
Ocean Boulevard

Danvers
Pickering Street

Hibiscus hedge
Prodigious flowers

Privet hedge
Small florets

Trabajadores contratados
Electric trimmers

Proprietor
Hand trimmer

Comparable discomfort
Under the sun

SAND

Sarasota sand
White
Powder

Palm Beach sand
Beige
Granular

Sarasota sand
In sandals
Hard to remove

Palm Beach sand
In sandals
Easy to wash out

Both
Florida sand

Southeast sand
My boyhood
Favorite

APPOINTMENT

Coconut palms
Strong sun
Puffy clouds
Mild breeze

Morning wavelets
Open shore
Clean sand

I've been
I'd be

But now
An appointment

TROLDHAUGEN

Erinnerungsmusik
Grieg's wedding day
By comparison
Un-noteworthy

Today and for some time

Bridesmaids
Stand in rows
Like pastel flowers
Powder blue or pink

Groomsmen
Aligned
Like cocktail waiters
Bow ties and tuxes

Music
Amplifiers
(Can there be music without amplifiers?)

Affluence
Affluence
Affluence

Poverty

MAGIC CARPET

Solomon's carpet
60 miles long
60 miles wide

As Wordsworth said
"I've measured it from side to side."

Rapid transport
A canopy of birds
Breakfast in Damascus
Sup in Media

Oriental fantasy

And now
An oriental carpet
At a yard sale

LUNCH UNDER AN UMBRELLA

A local grille
A patio
Tables and umbrellas
Shade

Artificial waterfall
Close by
A cascade
A serenade

A background
For lunch
Salmon salad
A glass of Riesling

Talk of this or that
Über alles mögliche
Civilized
North shore

BUDDHA BODHISSATVA

Buddha
Bodhissatva

Erhabener
Oder Jünger

Hesse told us

Not:
All is one

Not:
One can lose all

But:

A lost one
Can be more so

WALKING TRISTAN

    I

Wagner's tragic hero?

No.

Herriot's rural scamp

Our pug

Hurried winter walks
Desultory spring and autumn walks
Slow summer walks

Dvorak composed
In Nature's Realm

Tristan composed
Personality
Until excited

By another dog

    II

Small dog
Ruff Ruff Ruff

ANGEL BLUSH

(A nod to *Paradise Lost*, VIII, 620–29)

Incorporeal — and yet a body
A body — and yet incorporeal

And so they blend, angelic stuff with stuff
Angelic, incorporeal and knowing

Known and knowing much as kissing kissed
Imago Dei and *imago Dei*

On earth, in Eden and our long history
Of loving loved, loved loving and decay

Not known to angel sort who rather know
Ineffable joy and

                      no gold band

COASTAL IDYLL

Sun allay the cares
Waves wash them away

All who open to you
All who let you carry

What no one can
Our work

Recline under a palm
Consider a frond

Ponder a sea grape
See a pelican

Plunge
And crop a fish

AFTER ALL

An epic poem that sang of Martins Ferry
And Florida, Yale, Harvard and the Alps

A biblical theology that spanned
God's covenants and righteousness and faith

Sonnets and minor poems that displayed
A colloquy of thoughts and memories

A book on God the poet and a book
On our first mother and her mortal choice

And other books and *Festschrift* contributions,
Some commentaries and some articles

And after all a memory of beauty
And hope

           beyond imagination

KEY CASAS

On Largo sometimes
And farther south

Islamorada
Duck Key
Marathon

Key Vaca
Boot Key
Boca Chica

Casas sobre pilotes

O crafty architect
Who would outwit

Huracán
El tridente de Poseidón

SCROLL UPON SCROLL

Scroll and scroll
Another scroll
Another

Homer
Sophocles
Callimachus (μέγα βιβλίον μέγα κακόν)

Horace
Vergil
P. Ovidius Naso

Dante
Petrarch

Milton
Wordsworth

Whitman
Pound
Eliot
Those three mutts
And all their fleas

And all
Flea journals

PENDULUM

Pendulum swing
Far right
Stop
Far left
Stop
Never stop
In the middle

DARK AND LIGHT

Dark hours
Dark days

Women and children
Rule over them

God said it
Isaiah wrote it

You have a cloak
Rule over this rubble

Nathless
A light

In the dark
Who sees it?

RAFT RENTAL

25¢ a half hour
Almost a fortune

Eleven-year old
Lake Worth beach

Drag a raft
Swim and pull

Chest high
Climb on board

Opportune wave
Glorious ride

My quarter
My effort

Not my wave
Not my ocean

A BURDEN, A GIFT

How can it be a burden
A burden
A burden

Carried in my heart
Carried in my mind
Carried in full hands

When it is a gift
A gift
A gift

Given by the heart
Given by the mind
Given by those hands?

WAVES

A photon
A wave

Course bent
By the sun

Course bent
Not space

Palm Beach ocean
Palm Beach wave

Course bent
By the sand

Course bent
Not space

BEACH BOY

A boy with a bucket
A boy with a spade

What matter what grade
And no shade

Damp sand
Easy to work

Glossy shells
Easy to pick

A bucket to collect
A bucket and spade to build

Under the sun

SEA SHELLS

Scotch bonnets small
Cowries

Small fighting conch
Cockles and muscles

Calico scallop
Kitten's paw

Bubble shell
Florida cone

Lightning whelk
Triton's trumpet

Frutti di mare
Summon me

And my pail
An apt collector

SAND CASTLES

Bucket and spade
Plastic

A boy's tools
Build a castle

A citadel
A city

Massive walls
Towers and turrets

Damp sand
Coherent

Dominion
Of a day

Against waves

SEA SHELLS AND SAND CASTLES

Old beach, blue Gulf
Better days

Two castles
One ruin

Fighting conch
Turrets

Moon shell
Windows

Cardita shell also
And southern quahog

A starfish
Accent

Fragments

Shored

www.ingramcontent.com/pod-product-compliance
Lightning Source LLC
LaVergne TN
LVHW051658080426
835511LV00017B/2619